Crocs and

Written by Teresa Heapy

Collins

At the nature reserve

Come and see what lives in
this huge nature reserve!

3

The reserve has beaches and deep valleys.

valley

It also has cliffs, woods, forests, rivers, mudflats and swamps.

mudflats

swamp

Getting around

The reserve is gigantic! It would take ages to walk around it.

Most visitors come by car or bus.

Noisy foxes

Flying foxes call to each other constantly. They roost in big, noisy groups in rainforests and swamps.

They make a lot of noise!

Secret turtles

Flatback turtles only lay their eggs on a few beaches.
One of these is near the reserve.

Scientists camp here to learn about the turtles.

Only a few people camp here at a time!

Croc spot!

There are crocodiles all over the park.

Crocodiles open their mouths to release heat. These reptiles can't sweat to cool down.

A crocodile thrashes the water with its powerful tail.

It snatches its food in its mighty jaws.

Fantastic birds

Egret

You can see egrets on a pond called the Anbangbang Billabong. Egrets catch fish by stabbing them with their bills.

I'm bird-watching!

16

Blue-winged kookaburra

bright feathers

A family of kookaburras can nest in the same tree for up to 15 years!

Rock art

But it's not just animals that live here. It's been home to people for over 65,000 years.

a painting of a ship

Look at this amazing rock art.

Some of the pictures are 20,000 years old!

This interesting painting shows a fish! It's like an X-ray!

Originally, clay was used to make paint.

One kind of red paint lasts the longest.

That's why most of the pictures are completely red! The other paints have worn away.

Look at my photos!

flying foxes

flatback turtles

crocodile

22

birds

pictures

23

Review: After reading

Use your assessment from hearing the children read to choose any GPCs, words or tricky words that need additional practice.

Read 1: Decoding

- Look together at **constantly** on page 8. Challenge the children to separate the syllables as they sound out the word. (*con-stant-ly*)
- Challenge the children to sound out these words in the same way too:

  gi-gan-tic   An-bang-bang

  o-rig-in-all-y   Bill-a-bong

  com-plete-ly

Read 2: Prosody

- Choose two double page spreads and model reading with expression to the children. Ask the children to have a go at reading the same pages with expression.
- Show the children how you use a different voice for the narrator's speech bubbles.

Read 3: Comprehension

- Turn to pages 22 and 23 and encourage the children to talk through the photos, explaining what they have learnt about each.
- For every question ask the children how they know the answer. Ask:
  - On pages 2 to 5, what makes this reserve special? (e.g. *It has lots of wildlife and its landscape has lots of different features.*)
  - On pages 8 and 9, do you think flying foxes are the same as the foxes that live on the ground? Why? (e.g. *No, because they rest in the trees, and they can fly/glide.*)
  - Why do crocodiles open their mouths on a hot day? (*to keep them cool because they can't sweat*)
  - On pages 18 to 21, why is the rock art mostly red? (e.g. *because the other colours usually fade first*)
  - Which chapter did you find the most interesting? Why?
- Explain to the children that this book is about Kakadu National Park in Australia.
- The beautiful rock art on pages 18, 19 and 21 was made by First Nations Australians, who have lived in the area for many thousands of years. The oldest paintings at Kakadu National Park are around 20,000 years old, and painting is still a very important part of First Nations Australians' culture and life.